Volunteer
Management 101

*How to Recruit and
Retain Volunteers*

Allen Madding
and Dan King

ISBN-13: 978-0-692-16910-0
Library of Congress Control Number: 2018909209

Cover design by Fistbump Media, LLC

Some of the anecdotal illustrations in this book are true to life and are included with the permission of the persons involved. All other illustrations are composites of real situations, and any resemblance to people living or dead is coincidental.

"You may be able to 'buy' a person's back with a paycheck, position, power, or fear, but a human being's genius, passion, loyalty, and tenacious creativity are volunteered only."

- David Marquet, former submarine commander, leadership expert, and author

Table of Contents

Introduction

Over the last 35 years, I have served as a volunteer and managed volunteers in many different organizations. Along the way, I have seen some incredible leaders demonstrate how to love their volunteers and create an environment where people love to serve. I have also seen some well-intentioned leaders who for one reason or another did not fully comprehend how to lead volunteers. Maybe they worked in Corporate America and assumed the same management techniques they learned and observed at work would automatically apply to managing volunteers, or maybe they didn't have any formal training in management and people skills - I don't know. But what I do know is that an employee will tolerate a certain amount of rebuke and tersely worded emails more readily than a volunteer.

An employee needs the paycheck to pay the rent, the mortgage, the car payment, student debt, the credit card bill, the utilities, and a host of other bills. Volunteers, on the other hand are not motivated by a paycheck to stick it out when the manager is chewing someone out or things get uncomfortable. The volunteer is simply motivated by making a difference and being a part of the organization. Their commitment hinges strictly on how vested they are with the vision and purpose of the organization. When it gets to be too much of a hassle to serve, when they begin to feel unappreciated, when they feel underutilized, or when they feel the commitment is too demanding, they will walk away - usually without any warning or explanation.

A manager of volunteers needs to be asking a lot of questions both of themselves and the volunteers.

"What is the particular job I need the volunteer to do?"

"Do we have a clearly defined job description that can properly set the volunteers' expectations for this job?"

"Why would someone want to volunteer to do this in the first place?"

"How can we make this opportunity something people would love to do?"

"How do we prevent burn out?"

"How do we demonstrate our appreciation?"

If these questions seem strange to consider, then we need to carefully examine our whole approach to managing our volunteers. Volunteers are investing in our organization when they sign up to serve. They are saying, "I believe enough in what this organization is doing to support it with my time." We need to respect their investment and use it wisely as if they were investing financially in our organization. Time is the most precious commodity. We are constantly hearing people complain about not having time to get things done and activities that consume too much of their time. If we are going to ask them to donate their time to volunteer, then we need to demonstrate our appreciation for that investment.

Thoughts from Dan King

I was in a mentoring session with a corporate VP when I was asked the question, "What do you believe about leading people?" The question came because I was questioning certain techniques that I didn't feel completely aligned with my Biblical worldview.

The result of that conversation became my first blog, *management by Goa*.

I studied the Scriptures with an eye out for what they taught me about leading people. I learned from Paul's instructions for the Church. I gleaned immeasurable wisdom from the Proverbs. And I approached the Judges and other early leader as if their stories were case studies on leadership.

The results were transformative for my work in a secular workplace and in my volunteer ministry in the church.

In the workplace, people often lead by position or title. Everyone else follow, quite simply, because they must. But in volunteer organizations (like church ministries) the people are there not out of obligation.

Just like me, they could walk away at any minute. They serve because they are passionate about what they are doing. So, leading in a volunteer organization is more about leveraging their passion, not about accomplishing some goal we might have (well, maybe when the two things align).

Interestingly, once I began to (somewhat) master the techniques I learned for leading in a volunteer organization, the skill translated well into a secular workplace. And they made me a different kind of leader. A leader who stood out from the pack and led not from a power position, but from a passion position.

My contributions to this book are pieces I originally wrote in the *management by God* blog (and elsewhere). I pray that they encourage you and inspire you to be a stronger leader no matter where you're at.

Sharing Your Vision

"Vision is the ability to see people, places, and things, not just the way they are, but the way they could be."

- Sam Adeyemi

The Value of Shared Vision

When you think of positive impact, you think of how to make the best team dynamic. When you think of a better team dynamic, you think of inter-team communication. You envision your team walking out the roles that make your dream a reality. The biggest initial task at hand is for you to figure out how to paint the picture of that dream into a simple message that you can repeat over and over to your team members in such a way that it invokes the same excitement in them that it does for you.

In his book, Leadership is an Art, Max Depree, former CEO of Herman Miller office furniture company, explains it by saying, "The first responsibility of a leader is to define reality." (DePree, 1987)

The absolute first step in recruiting a volunteer is to clearly communicate the organization's Vision, Purpose, Mission, and Goals. Founders and boards of directors spend countless hours wrangling, sculpting, and defining these foundational elements of an organization. They keeps everyone moving in the same direction. Without clearly defined and communicated vision, everyone in the organization will wander aimlessly in what they think they should be trying to accomplish, and volunteers will become quickly frustrated in the lack of direction. Our job as a volunteer leader is to effectively translate the vision into something tangible - something the volunteers can taste, feel, and yearn to walk out.

Years ago, I served as the IT Director for a church. Several of the staff members needed training on different office products that they had never used. Some wanted to learn to write spreadsheet macros, others wanted to learn to create PowerPoint presentations, and others wanted to learn to perform word processing mail merges. I had so many projects going as well as the day-to-day general support responsibilities, I decided to recruit some volunteers who used those products day in and day out to provide the staff with one-on-one training.

So, when the annual volunteer drive came along, I advertised for the positions. The church held a night time event that allowed members who were interested in serving to meet with staff members and hear about the positions. The first year for me was a total flop. When I began to review what went wrong, it became obvious to me that it was solely my fault that no one had signed up to serve as an IT volunteer. What had I done wrong? I didn't effectively communicate my vision to the people that stopped in that night to ask about the positions.

The second year, I was prepared. I had the positions clearly defined, and I worked on clear explanations of the vision of the team and each position. About a half dozen or so people stopped by the Sunday School classroom I was sitting in that night. They asked for more information. I explained what the staff was desiring. I then explained that all of the staff worked very hard, but many were not fully utilizing the tools that were available to them because of the lack of training.

I then communicated the vision: "My vision is a team of volunteers who can come alongside the staff members and help them learn to use many of

vision

the office products that are installed on their computers that many business people use every day. By training the staff on these tools, we will bless them with the ability to work smarter instead of harder and become to more productive."

"I would like to have a Volunteer Training Coordinator. This person would have the contact information for every volunteer trainer and what their areas of specialty are. When I receive a request from a staff member for training, I will communicate that information to the Training Coordinator. They will then contact volunteer trainers who are skilled in that area and check their availability. The available trainer will then contact the staff member and set up a time to provide desk-side one-on-one training," I explained.

The whole group looked at me in amazement and said, "That sounds easy. We could do that!"

One person began rattling off what she had experience with - word processor templates, preparing mailing labels, mail merges, etc. Another began rattling off his expertise - spreadsheet formulas, pivot tables, custom reporting. A third shared she spent the majority of her work week preparing videos and PowerPoint shows.

Within an hour, I had a Volunteer Training Coordinator and six or seven Volunteer IT Trainers. I walked out amazed and thrilled with the results. I had the same vision for the team walking into that classroom that night that I had the year before with extremely different results. The difference in the failure of the first year and the success of the second year was simple - effectively communicating the vision!

"Great leaders communicate a vision that captures the imagination and fires the hearts and minds of those around them."

- Joseph B. Wirthlin, American businessman, religious leader

My explanation during the first year had fallen flat. The people that stopped by to inquire could not see themselves performing those roles, and they didn't see the value from volunteering. My explanation the second year stirred their imaginations. Each one could see themselves using their skills to assist the staff in being able to work smarter rather than harder and thereby reducing their daily job stress.

"True leadership isn't about having an idea. It's about having an idea and recruiting other people to execute on this vision."

- Leila Janah, CEO of Samasource and LXMI

In year one, the problem was clear to me, as was the solution. I did not have the bandwidth to personally provide custom tailored individual training to 65 staff members and perform the rest of my daily and weekly duties, so recruiting volunteers to assist was a brilliant idea. But I failed to recruit people to execute the idea. We had a failure to launch. Year two was the exact same idea from year one. The difference was in the communication of the vision. I effectively translated the vision into something tangible and by doing so, I was able to recruit people to execute that vision.

"Good business leaders create a vision, articulate the vision, passionately own the vision, and relentlessly drive it to completion."

- Jack Welch, former chairman and CEO of General Electric

Executing the Vision

After finally communicating the vision, I still had to take ownership. I didn't just say, "Hey great, we have a team. They can take the ball and run with it. I will check in on them next year." Nope. I had to own it and continue to drive it. The following week, I emailed everyone that attended that night and thanked them for volunteering. I communicated next steps and stayed in contact. I relayed the current training requests already on hand, and then communicated to the staff that a team of volunteers were ready and waiting to provide training to them.

When I didn't get a response on a request, as in you could hear crickets in my email inbox, I followed up. A quick phone call beats sitting and wondering what went wrong. Did someone get burned out, is someone ill, did someone get offended, was there a death in the family? I continued to own the vision and drive it to completion. By the end of the year, half of the staff were utilizing the volunteer IT trainers and were raving about their experiences to the other staff members.

Why is effectively communicating the vision so important? The everyday mundane tasks can become boring and volunteers can lose their interest if they don't see how their piece fits in the overall big picture. As leaders, we have a clear understanding of the importance of the roles each volunteer makes towards our overall objective. But the folks down in the trenches don't always see that clearly. If you are volunteering in the parking lot in freezing rain or sleet with cars spraying you with slush as they pass, you can quickly forget the importance of your role in making guests feel welcome and less overwhelmed with the parking arrangements of a new environment.

Conversely, a volunteer that sees and understands how their contribution positively affects the lives of those they meet will be motivated to serve and will continue to be back week after week. And those volunteers are the ones that bring friends and neighbors to come serve with them. Current volunteers can become your best recruiting tool for additional volunteers.

"I believe to be a leader is to enable others to embrace a vision, initiative or assignment in a way that they feel a sense of purpose, ownership, personal engagement, and common cause. I was very affected as a child by my father's positive example as a civic leader who inspired others to share his commitment to improving our community."

- Melanne Verveer, Executive Director of the Georgetown Institute for Women, Hillary Clinton's former chief of staff

By effectively communicating the vision, we enable the volunteers to embrace it. When they embrace it, they develop a sense of ownership - they can see they are making a positive impact in their community. When they see they are positively impacting the community, they begin to realize their purpose. Do you see how fantastic it is to help someone realize their purpose? Most people wander through life searching for their purpose. As leaders, we are giving a gift to our volunteer teams when we help them understand and embrace the vision, because we are helping them find their purpose.

"Leadership is about vision and responsibility, not power."

- Seth Berkley, President and CEO of the International AIDS Vaccine Initiative

Growing up watching world leaders, military leaders, and business leaders, we form an opinion that leadership is one thing: POWER. In school, we study great leaders like George Washington, Abraham Lincoln, George Patton, Douglas McArthur, and Winston Churchill, and we are in awe of the power they exercised. Our take away is a great leader is powerful. So, to become powerful, we need to become a leader. That is the farthest from the truth! Leadership is not about empowering yourself, it's about empowering other people. Leadership is taking responsibility for a team and effectively communicating vision. When the team begins to stray off course, we guide them back to the vision.

In his book, Servant Leadership, the late Robert Greenleaf, founder of the modern servant leadership movement and the Greenleaf Center for Servant Leadership, talks about how leaders embrace goals.

"As long as one is leading, one always has a goal. It may be a goal arrived at by group consensus, or the leader, acting on inspiration, may have simply said, 'Let's go this way.' But the leader always knows what it is and can articulate it for any who are unsure. By clearly stating and restating the goal, the leader gives certainty to others who may have difficulty in achieving it for themselves." (Greenleaf, 1977)

Greenleaf then defines goal in this sense as *"the overarching purpose, the big dream, the visionary concept..."* (Greenleaf, 1977)

"It's necessary to know that everybody won't see it. That everybody won't join you, that everybody won't have the vision. It's necessary to know that. That a lot of people like to complain but they don't want to do anything about their situation. That you are UNCOMMON breed."

- Les Brown, motivational speaker, author, radio DJ, former television host, and former member of the Ohio House of Representatives

When Someone Doesn't Get the Vision

Do your best to communicate the vision and help people embrace the vision, but do not become overwhelmed when you encounter the folks that just cannot see the vision if you draw it out in color for them. You are going to encounter them, and if you are not expecting it, it can be overwhelming and discouraging. Not everyone you approach and invest in will see the vision and embrace it. The first one you encounter will probably take your breath away. It may feel like someone punched you blindsided. Do not let it derail you. Press on! Someone is going to listen to you communicate the vision, and they are going to respond with something like, "That just isn't in my wheelhouse." Do not allow it to wound you or distract you. Chalk it up that they are just not at a place in their journey to take this step, and then move along.

The Rally Point (Dan King)

Remember the scene in *Braveheart* when Mel Gibson's character, William Wallace, was giving the freedom speech just before the big battle? I've often wondered what it takes to be such a leader. It would be really cool to be able to rally people the way that William Wallace did. Imagine the influence it would require to motivate people to give their lives for a cause.

However, even though today's organizations aren't faced with a need for *that* strong of a commitment, we often fight for our lives against detractors flying in our faces who would love nothing more than to see us fall.

There was a time in the early days of the nation of Israel that an oppression took over. If the nation were to survive, then it would need someone to step up and lead them. But before we talk about this seldom heard of leader, let's lay the groundwork first...

In the history of Israel, there was a time that the nation was virtually leaderless. There was little to no governing authority. People simply lived in the territories of each of the 12 tribes that made up Israel. This time was after the occupation of the land of Canaan. But even before that, the "nation" had been in bondage in Egypt for hundreds of years.

Most of their identity was wrapped up in the promise of being a great nation, all the while they're living under the rule of another "world power". Eventually, they're delivered from bondage, and witnessed great miracles in the process (like the crossing of the Red Sea). However, this newly delivered nation wandered in the desert for 40 years before taking over the promised land.

Think about this fact for a moment.

All of the men of fighting age are either dead or too old to fight by the time they get to enter the promised land. So all of the great warriors are the young men that were born in the desert, and simply missed witnessing the miracle of the Exodus.

So, this new generation enters the promised land, and they take over and settle into their new homes. Remember, this is mostly a generation that is inheriting the promise from their forefathers and have only heard stories about some of the greatest miracles that ever happened. So, they get in and get comfortable.

Have you ever been a part of an organization that has gotten "comfortable" where it is at? I believe that often some of our biggest problems come from accepting the status quo.

As the nation of Israel got comfortable, they started fulfilling their own will rather than seeking the will of God (their ultimate Authority).

Imagine what this would look like in today's environment. Think about people who do things that don't seem to be quite in alignment with what the organization wants to accomplish. Often these people are very much about doing what they think is best for them, but if you're someone concerned about taking the organization in a specific direction, you may be wondering what the heck is wrong with them. Well, this is pretty much the situation in Israel, and it got them taken over by a foreign ruler for about eight years until someone got fed up with it...

Enter Othniel. God raised up a man to judge Israel and kick out this foreign king. If you look closely at the record of this time, you'll notice that two major things happened, and in a specific order.

First, Othniel, with "the Spirit of the Lord upon him" (or the Power of God's Authority delegated to him) "judged Israel."

In other words, as a representative of The Leader, he enforced the plans of the organization.

He held people accountable to the tasks that they were responsible for.

Part of me cannot help but to think of Sylvester Stallone's character of Judge Dredd where the "judges" acted as police, judge, jury, and executioner right there. I don't know that it was that extreme in Othniel's time, but I do know that he had a little house-cleaning to do before he could get anywhere.

Sometimes we need to enforce (or reinforce) expectations before any other foreign enemy can be dealt with.

After that, he "went out to war". Some of the traditions that were recorded by Josephus indicate that, "with a few other brave men, he massacred one of the Assyrian garrisons." For the non-military types reading this, a garrison is a fortified military unit. So basically, we're talking about how a few "brave" men took on an Army unit in a well-protected fort. This must have been a pretty formidable task, and a major feat to accomplish.

Josephus continues by saying that, "when the Israelites saw that he had been successful in his first attempt, they rallied around him in great numbers."

Once complete victory had been achieved, there was peace and rest in the land for the next 40 years, until Othniel's death. When I read this, I cannot help but to think that Othniel led the people with his actions. He moved in power and proved to the people that he was not afraid to get his hands dirty.

I think that there are several modern-day business world implications here. Most importantly, we need to recognize (and hopefully prevent) complacency from setting in. If we are to continue to win the fight for survival, then comfort and self-seeking motives have no place in our organizations. If complacency is setting in, what can you do as a leader to remind people of the mission and hold them accountable for their part in it? Further, how can you "get your hands dirty' and lead by example to show people not only that it can be done, but also *how* it can be done?

Going back to the opening example of William Wallace, he also proved himself in the smaller battles as being worth following into the big ones. In the same way, Othniel made his presence known, and as long as he was alive his presence was also felt. Ask yourself what you can learn from Othniel's life to be a leader who can rally the troops when needed.

Questions to Consider

- How can I effectively translate our organization's vision to our volunteers so that they can taste, feel, and yearn to walk it out?

- How can I communicate the vision regularly (Perhaps weekly?) to our volunteers so that it is something they know and can communicate to others?

- If someone stopped me in the hall right now, could I communicate our vision to them without having to think about it?

- Has our organization become complacent? Are we comfortable where we are, or are we pushing forward towards our vision?

- How can you "get your hands dirty", and lead by example to show people not only that it can be done, but also *how* it can be done?

- Is anyone or any group doing things that don't seem to be in alignment with what the organization wants to accomplish? If so, how can we re-align them with the vision?

Providing Opportunity

Once you clearly embrace the vision of your organization, you need to begin creating an inventory of opportunity for volunteers to serve. Leader burn out is a direct result of trying to do everything and overextending. It is far better to do a few things with excellence than many things with mediocrity. We call this going deep instead of going wide. Identify the tasks that need to be accomplished and then create roles for the tasks. Once you have clearly defined roles, you can begin recruiting for those roles. Set solid goals for each role and clearly communicate those goals with the volunteers that serve in those roles. Then keep communicating with them.

Do you know someone who quit volunteering with an organization or a ministry? Ask them why they quit, and you will get several different answers. One that comes up time and again is, "It wasn't what I was expecting." Effective communication can eliminate this problem. The best time to prevent that from happening is on day one. Give a potential volunteer a good idea of what to expect, helping them make an informed commitment to the position. Be honest with them. Don't sugar coat things and set expectations that will never be met. A potential volunteer will quickly begin to respect a leader who is upfront and honest with them.

If you are approached to drive a truck to collect surplus food for a food pantry, you would appreciate being told that there will be some heavy lifting, you might get dirty and sweaty, and you really need to feel comfortable driving and backing up a truck with a big box on the back. On the other hand, if you are given the keys to a large refrigerated box truck and handed directions to a restaurant and you have never driven anything bigger than a Smart Car, you might decide to quit on day one.

Someone might say "But Allen, if we tell them the dirty details of the job, no one will volunteer for the job." I disagree. It might, however, take you a little longer to find someone to volunteer for the role, but when you do, the chances are significantly higher they will reflect on their first day's experience with a positive outlook and then return for a second day. My experience is that it is better to wait for a volunteer who is willing to take on a role and who fully understands all aspects - good and bad - than to just put butts in seats. If you recruit a volunteer who doesn't understand what they are getting into, they will quit in short order. Consequently, you will spend all of your time and effort in constantly trying to backfill positions. Tell them upfront, "You will encounter some less than grateful people as you distribute food. Understand they are at a bad time in their lives. Love them, smile at them, do the right thing, and serve the next person." Openness and honesty will earn you a ton of respect and loyalty with your volunteers. When they encounter an uncomfortable or difficult task or situation, they will think to themselves, "Well, they did tell me this would happen. Glad they gave me forewarning."

Another aspect of providing opportunity is providing the volunteers with the opportunity to to improve processes. The volunteers are the ones on the front lines having daily or weekly contact with the people served. They have a front row seat for what works and what doesn't work. They are our best sources of feedback on what does and doesn't work. Do not, let me say this again, DO NOT make changes without consulting the volunteers first. No one likes to be blindsided. Don't walk into your cafe while they are setting up for the event and say, "Oh by the way, I've decided to change the way y'all distribute coffee and doughnuts." Unless of course you really don't like your volunteers and want them all to quit. Instead, meet with them and say, "What do y'all think of changing the way you distribute coffee and doughnuts at events?" Describe your thoughts and then ask for their input. Carefully listen to their responses. Don't write them off as resistant to change. Listen! They are the ones that pay the price if your idea is a flop, so allow their input. Be flexible enough to consider modifying your new plan and allow them a hand in redesigning the service they provide.

Finally, if we are going to provide opportunity, we need to provide opportunity to lead and change roles. The first volunteer to serve in a particular role does not automatically become the best candidate to lead a team. Observe the team. Who is the problem solver? Who is dependable? Who is setting a great example of a servant-leader? Who is the encourager? Who does the team seem to automatically follow?

Watch for volunteers that don't seem to be a perfect match for the role they are in and consider where they might be a better fit. Allow them the opportunity to try another role on another team. Consider that some roles might be the "toes in the water" role, which is a role that anyone can step into easily as a first step in volunteering. Consider that after a year or two, some of those volunteers might consider taking on a new role. Not everyone is going to jump at the opportunity to lead a small group of middle school boys. But how about a role as a greeter, a role in the parking team, or serving in the Cafe?

I remember vividly my 4th week attending a church in an Atlanta suburb straight out of college. I was asked to teach Children's Sunday School. I agreed since I had worked four summers as a youth director. What I didn't know was there was no rotation and no backups. It was a 52 Sunday per year commitment with no relief in sight. No opportunity for me to attend a young adult class, no opportunity for me to change roles after a year. I was placed and expected to serve there until death I guess. So when I bought my first house and moved to the other side of town, you shouldn't be surprised to learn that I found another church and ended my service in the Children's Sunday School. Looking back, I should have probably put up a smoke signal, phoned a friend or discussed the impending burn out with someone, but I was 22 and was ready to bail.

Don't let that happen on your watch. Recognize it is a possibility. Recognize the commitment you are asking and provide opportunities for your volunteers to take a break or to change roles. Many volunteers will serve your organization for years if they recognize they have opportunities to change roles when they begin feeling burned out.

Questions to Consider

- What opportunities currently exist in our organization where volunteers could serve and make a difference?
- Have we clearly defined roles addressing these opportunities?
- Have we set solid goals for each role?
- Have we clearly communicated those goals with the volunteers that serve in those roles?
- How do we ensure that volunteers in these roles do not burn out and can take a break when they need?

Training

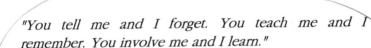

"You tell me and I forget. You teach me and I remember. You involve me and I learn."

- Benjamin Franklin

The Importance of Training

Several years ago, I bought a small farm outside a rural town in South Georgia. I frequented a small country store up the road a few miles which saved me the long drive into town. One day the owner mentioned they had a volunteer fire department and asked me to consider volunteering. A month or so later, I stopped in for their monthly volunteer meeting. They were friendly and welcoming. They showed me around the trucks and gave me a radio. The next afternoon, I got a call to provide mutual aide to a neighboring community. I had ZERO training in firefighting. I drove down to the station, rolled up the door, and started the truck. Another guy around 19 or 20 rolled up and jumped in the passenger side of the truck. We called the dispatcher on the radio and requested directions and off we went to my first fire. On the way, we heard radio traffic from the crew on scene: "It's a big, big fire!" was the assessment we heard.

After two or three wrong turns we arrived on scene to see a garage with flames licking the sky, a downed live power line, and paint cans that were building pressure and intermittently blowing their lids into the air. A seasoned volunteer rolled up fully dressed in bunker gear, helmet, gloves, and boots. I was in blue jeans, cowboy boots and a short sleeve work shirt. He fired up the pump, pulled a hose, and began attacking the fire. I backed him up handling the hose. After a few minutes I could feel a light electrical tingle. He quickly recognized what was happening, shut off the nozzle and tossed the hose down. We had drug the hose across the downed live power line. Fire hoses seep or sweat water and it was just enough to send an electrical charge all the way up the hose and was shocking us. He managed to get the hose moved away from the power line, and we resumed our attack. Suddenly, there was a loud boom, and I hit the dirt. After taking a full inventory of my limbs, I realized an air compressor had built up pressure from the heat and had blown a pop-off valve. When the fire was extinguished and we headed back to the station, thoughts ran through my mind of how unprepared I was for what I just experienced. Chalk it up to young and dumb or the sense of adventure, but I didn't quit. I would bet many volunteers would have hung it up after that experience for a first day. It was another three or four months before an opportunity arose for me to attend basic firefighter training and become certified. Looking back, maybe I was "certifiable" for sticking around after literally being thrown in the fire on day one. Would you have returned to a volunteer role after that kind of introduction?

Do you see places in your organization where new volunteers are thrust into the role without adequate (or any) training? Provide training for your new volunteers so they can become comfortable in their roles. Don't throw them in the fire on the first day. Let them be mentored by someone who has been performing that role for a month, so they can ease into the position. Provide them solutions to "what if" scenarios. Every volunteer role has them. What if the parking lot completely fills and we still have cars coming in to park? Where do we send the overflow? What if the first service runs long and cars start arriving before the parking lot has begun emptying? Where do we send the arrivals until the main lot is available? What if a disabled person needs assistance with a wheelchair? What entrance to the building has wheelchair access? What if someone has a flat?

What if someone needs a jump start? What happens when the fire truck runs out of water? Who do you call if you're sick and can't serve during your rotation? While you will never be able to completely prepare and address every possibility, strive to have set answers for the majority of the what-ifs? Even if the volunteers aren't asking them, they are thinking them.

I watch NASCAR racing a good bit and recognize the teams spend a lot of time and money properly training and preparing their pit crews so that they can make lightning fast pit stops. The race car slides to a stop and six guys go over the wall, one guy pumps a jack while two others remove the right-side wheels. As they pull the wheels off, a tire carrier has run around the car carrying two new tires and they throw them on the wheel studs and hit the lug nuts with their air guns to tighten them down. The jack man drops the jack and swings around to the other side of the car, jacks that side of the car into the air while the tire changers pull those wheels off. Again in perfect timing, the tire carrier delivers two new tires and helps get them set on the wheel studs. And again the tire changers hit the lugnuts with their air guns to tighten them down. While all of this has been going on another guy has a heavy fuel can up on his shoulder and connects it to a fuel inlet at the rear fender and is refilling the fuel tank. The jack drops and everyone dashes for the pit wall while the car smokes the tires heading out of the pits and back onto the racetrack. The crews with the fastest pit stop win the battle on pit road to have their car back out on the track first. A competitive pit stop is completed in under 12 seconds. Anything slower, and you have hurt your team's chances for a win that day. Races have been won and lost on pit road. The success there comes down to training, and the teams practice these stops during the week. But just training and practicing for the pit stop isn't enough. What if the car is damaged in a wreck? Recently NASCAR implemented a rule that teams would have a maximum of five minutes to repair a car to a level that it could run a minimum speed on the track. If after five minutes the car was not able to return to the track or if it was unable to maintain a minimum speed on the track, they were disqualified from continuing to compete for the day. Not finishing an event is a huge hit to a team that is seeking to win the season championship. So as you might imagine, the crew chiefs also work to prepare the teams for working under the five minute clock.

This past weekend I was watching one of the races and a driver who was on the cusp of making the next round of the playoff championship was involved in a wreck and required repair. He brought the car onto pit road to the attention of his pit crew. They jumped over the wall and worked feverishly to repair the damage within the five-minute window and well enough to meet the minimum speed requirement when the car returned to competition. As the car returned to the track, NASCAR noted that seven crew members had went over the wall to effect repairs, and they were disqualified from competing in the remainder of the event. The team lost enough points from failing to complete the entire race which resulted in elimination from the championship playoff format. After the race was over, television reporters questioned the driver and the crew chief on what happened. The driver was confused as to the rule understandably as it is not the driver's responsibility to know all of the rules pertaining to the pit crew. When they interviewed the crew chief, he quickly explained that he was fully aware that only six crew members could work to repair a car under the five-minute clock rule. He said that he had directed six crew members but, "somebody couldn't count." Sorry folks, but the crew chief is the leader of that team and is solely responsible for ensuring they know what is expected and what the rules are in those situations. Before the car entered pit road, the crew chief should have been on the radio reminding them, "We're under the five-minute clock, so we can only have six people over the wall. The six people are Jackson, Murphy, Smith, Davis..." The misunderstanding that happened in those few minutes eliminated that team from a chance at a championship, and the leader should have assumed the responsibility.

As a leader of volunteers, we don't have the luxury of practicing multiple times a week, if any at all. We have to give careful attention to training our teams and asking for feedback.

Teaching and Training (Dan King)

Once when I was really young, I remember that I wanted to take an apple to one of my grade-school teachers. I don't remember much about the circumstances, but I do remember certain feelings about the event. I know that the whole apple thing is very cliché, but to me as a young boy, I wanted to do something for the teacher who made me happy.

How did she make me happy? By helping me to learn something. To me learning always felt good. And I've always had a great deal of respect for the people who've helped me to learn something new.

As we consider training, we come across the requirement of leaders being able to teach.

This one is very near and dear to me, because my profession in the workplace today is in the Learning and Development field. I also feel that this is God's call on my life. I've lead a young adult ministry at the church that I attend, and I teach regularly with our church's school of ministry. I am a teacher and trainer down to the bone, so I couldn't wait to write about this topic!

First, I want to talk about the importance of this skill. Often in the workplace, the responsibility for teaching people is left up to the "training department". And when there are problems, many often point out that it is a "training issue" and pass the responsibility off to someone else.

But the important thing to consider here is that developing people is the responsibility of *every* leader, and not just the training department.

Why? Because as the leader you are responsible for the success of the vision. Therefore, you are also responsible for ensuring that the people have the tools and skills needed to achieve that vision. This especially holds true for the people who are closest to you in the reporting structure. You should always be grooming people to move up.

In regard to teaching, there's a lot of great information out there about how to reach people and have a lasting impact. However, there are a couple of key ideas that I believe are most important to your success as a "teacher".

 First of all, you must consider it *your* responsibility to ensure that the learning happened.

Anyone can share information, but a great teacher is one who ensures that it actually sinks in. It's true that the learner has a responsibility to learn, but don't count on the fact that they think the same way you do. Take it upon yourself to try different approaches, and don't stop until you're sure that they "get it". This leads me to my next point…

Secondly, you must understand that people learn differently.

People have different learning styles. Simply put, you cannot expect someone who is a visual learner (likes reading, pictures) to learn effectively by telling them the steps that they need to follow. Even if you're lecturing to the visual learner, you must understand that you need to speak in visual terms… "Imagine a speed boat and a tug boat. This is like your…".

Typically, there are a few standard types of learning styles (visual, auditory, tactual, and kinesthetic). If you understand them well, you can even tell what learning style a person is simply by observing their body language. Often, people will tell you how they learn best (even if they do not understand "learning styles").

The point is that you need to know how your people learn and take this into consideration when you teach them. Don't get frustrated because one person can't seem to follow verbal instructions the way someone else does. You just may not be communicating to them in a "language" that they understand.

As a leader, *YOU* are responsible for your volunteers' success.

Therefore, it's important to invest in them. I've always believed that not only should each of us seek out a mentor in order to develop ourselves, but we should look to mentor someone else as well.

One thing that you'll discover when you sow into someone else's success is that they'll follow you anywhere. There are few things that build a person's self-esteem better than investing in their success. It not only makes them feel good about themselves, but also about you.

Questions to Consider

- What are you doing to develop the people on your team?

- If you moved on to bigger and better things, who would you select to replace you?

- Why did you pick that person?

- Are they fully equipped to handle your job?

- What do you need to be teaching them that you currently are not?

- What do they want to learn?

- How can you better contribute to the development required to allow them the growth that they desire?

- How are you learning to be a better teacher?

- Think of your next in line volunteer leader. Do you know his/her learning style? What resources can you use to figure out how to speak in a way that suits his/her learning?

Equipping

Equip the volunteers so they can succeed at what you are asking them to do. Set them up for success! When that fire was roaring that day on my first fire scene, I would have really loved to have had a set of bunker gear, gloves, and a helmet. When I was getting shocked holding the hose, I would have loved to have had a pair of rubber boots. How different would that experience have been if I had been equipped properly? What kind of impression does an organization make on volunteers when they are ill-equipped to perform the task set before them? Just because we operate in a non-profit space doesn't mean that we are given a free pass for being unprepared and unprofessional. Volunteers will gladly continue to serve in an organization that feels like they have their stuff together. Conversely, continue to put them in uncomfortable positions where we are constantly flying by the seat of our pants, and they will grow tired of the frustration and quit.

Granted, things happen. Plans fall through and communication fails. When it does, be prepared to step up, claim responsibility, apologize, and make a concerted effort to keep it from happening again. Volunteers can withstand an occasional failure, but not the same repeated failures. Volunteers can't be expected to pay for our mistakes. It shouldn't be on their shoulders to correct. Step in, correct it, and move forward with lessons learned.

Consider each role you plan to fill and then begin to answer the question: "How could we best equip a volunteer to be successful in this role?" Sure, handing out t-shirts is all fine and good. But if you are staffing a parking team, consider providing rain gear, shade hats for summer, and high visibility vests to ensure they are seen. Consider providing radios so they can communicate between themselves as well as request assistance. Maybe provide them with a floor jack and a lug wrench so they can change a flat tire. Maybe provide them a jump box for helping guests when their car won't start. If it is a hot summer day, consider providing bottles of cold water to the team.

If you are staffing a position in the bookstore, are all the items priced so the volunteer understands how much to charge for each item? Do the clothing items have clear size tags? Have you demonstrated how to accept credit/debit cards? Is there a back-up tablet or computer if the one being utilized crashes or begins loading an update that makes it unavailable for a long period of time? Is there sufficient change in the cash box? If items are in storage containers, are the storage containers clearly marked with the item description and size, if applicable?

Check in with the teams in each of the areas where they serve and ask what the frustrations are that they encounter. Consider what alternatives are available to alleviate those frustrations. If the bookstore software is not intuitive, is there some other software we could utilize?

Provide volunteers the means to work effectively and minimize unnecessary frustrations. Set them up for success so they don't feel like they have been set up. Their success is your success.

Questions to Consider

- What does each team of volunteers need to be properly equipped?
- Have we set up our volunteers to succeed?
- What is frustrating our volunteers? If you do or don't know, ask them!
- How can we eliminate the frustration?

Supporting

Once your team has been trained and equipped, support them. Chances are, you manage more than one team and have a lot of responsibilities. Trust me. I get it. But your volunteers need your support. Make time in the hectic day to day to check in with each team and ideally each team member if just for a minute and ask them how they are or if they need anything. For extra credit on scorching hot summer days with volunteers working outside, occasionally have a box of ice cream sandwiches waiting in a nearby freezer or cooler when they come in from serving. Supporting your volunteers will earn you respect and loyalty faster than anything else you can do. After an hour in 90 degree heat standing in the middle of an asphalt parking lot, there is nothing I appreciate more than seeing someone walking towards me carrying ice cold bottles of water. It is the little things that carry the most weight. It is a nonverbal communication that says, "I am grateful for your service, I appreciate you, and I value you."

If you don't support your volunteers, they will hang with you for a short period of time and move on somewhere else where a leader supports them and they feel valued and appreciated. Take a look at the volunteers and teams you have serving with you and consider how you can support them and make them feel valued.

The Core of Leadership is Hope (Dan King)

In her book, *Unleashing the Power of Rubber Bands: Lessons in Non-linear Leadership,* Nancy Ortberg states that she believes that the core of leadership is "hope."

At first I didn't quite get the point. I sat in my reading chair thinking, "hmmm… interesting perspective, but it'll never fly in the real world." But then as I read on and got drawn in by her argument to this point, I started to get it. By the end of the chapter, I was like… **"duh… the core of leadership is *hope*!"**

In a nutshell, leaders have the task of giving people hope. Ortberg says, "Leadership is the hope that we can change the things that need to be changed and create what we cannot now imagine… Hope dispels fears. Hope readies us for round two." I could go on, but I'll let you get the book to read more about what Ortberg says.

This got me thinking about what it means to me to be a leader. In the workplace, it means that I should **build up and encourage others**. Help them by holding up their arms and getting them through difficult and challenging times. In my ministry, it means that I'm **supporting others in discovering who they are in Christ** and what God has made them to do. It also means that in the ministry we spend less time getting comfortable in our Bible studies, and more time getting out to **give others in our community hope** as well.

It's even challenged me to think about other things that I can do to spread hope.

I was recently talking to some friends from Zimbabwe. Just before they were set to return to their home country, we talked about what's needed most over there. In case you aren't aware, the economy there is in shambles. Inflation is in the millions of percent, and unemployment is 90-95%. These are conditions that most of us would have a difficult time even imagining. My friend tells me that the people *want* to work, but the jobs just aren't there. He also tells me that the biggest need is to help these people get started in some sort of business that they could do on their own. Even something as simple as a sewing machine will help someone to create work in making clothing that they can sell locally.

It sounds to me like there's an **opportunity to create hope** there.

Questions to Consider

- How can we demonstrate our support to our volunteers?
- How can we ensure the volunteers feel valued?
- What can we do to hold up our volunteers' arms to get them through difficult times?
- How can we build up and encourage our volunteers?
- How can we communicate that what we do makes a difference?

How can we support our volunteers to proactively identify problems and solutions?

Being Flexible

One of the hardest tasks you will undertake managing volunteers will be balancing the needs of your volunteers against the needs of the organization. Maneuvering this virtual mine field can make or break your teams and eventually your organization. Your volunteers are people trying to balance the demands of their jobs, their families, their personal lives, and their commitment to your organization. We have to keep in mind that life happens, and it happens at the least opportune times. Family members die, a volunteer's child gets the flu, and people have to drop plans and commitments in a moment's notice to attend to arrangements. Family members become ill or injured and require someone to be with them at the hospital. Jobs suddenly demand change of work schedules that conflict with volunteer commitments, and important work projects may require overtime.

As successful managers, we have to understand these challenges will crop up, and we should expect them. We have to somehow be prepared for the unexpected. How in the world do we do that? Glad you asked! By being flexible and asking our volunteers to be flexible. When these types of situations arise, stay calm and consider the options. Can we ask a volunteer that is on a different schedule if they can cover? Can we ask a greeter to fill in on the parking team? Can we ask a parking team member to fill in as an usher? And in the worst-case scenario, we roll up our sleeves and fill the position ourselves.

Accept and embrace the truth that an individual volunteer's ability to commit may change over time. Do not fall into the expectation that someone serving in the parking lot will want to stay on that team for ten years. Granted, some might. But others might have committed to that team as an entry point - to get their feet wet volunteering and see how it goes. After a year or two, they might be wanting to step up into another role. Maybe they want to usher or serve in the children's ministry. Be expecting it so it doesn't surprise you, and make plans to accommodate it when it does.

Accept and embrace that a volunteer may find out their talents are better suited for a different role than the one they originally accepted. Be observant and note what talents your volunteers are demonstrating that are not currently being harnessed. When you talk with them during down time, what are their interests outside the organization? If you have a firefighter that is well spoken, he or she may be an excellent choice for interacting with the press. If someone is a writer, they could be an excellent candidate for writing press releases or grant writing. You may very well have someone underutilized sitting right in front of you every week and not even realize it. How will you find out? By interacting with each member of the team, listening intently to everything they talk about - even small talk, and observing them in action.

Providing an Exit

When the unexpected arises, provide volunteers the opportunity for a "leave of absence". Sometimes people need the opportunity to step away from their responsibilities in order to physically, mentally and emotionally recover. We need to be gracious enough to offer them that opportunity when they need it. Some of the hardest moments of life require changing focus for a period of time and just dealing with the issue that has arisen. Even in the good times, everyone deserves to take some time off for family vacation, family reunion, anniversaries, moving, downtime, etc. Many may refuse the offer, but we need to provide it and be flexible enough to find ways to cover their spots and let them catch their breath.

Allow volunteers to leave gracefully without feeling guilty. Remember my story earlier about the Children's Sunday School Class? It would have been great had there been an expiration date on the commitment or an understood length. I have seen churches do an amazing job of doing this by communicating a length of commitment up front. When they recruit for Middle School Small Group Leaders, they clearly communicate it is a three-year commitment so the leaders remain with the students through their middle school experience. At the end of the three years, the leadership meets with the volunteers and inquires if they would like to commit for another three years of new middle schoolers, if they would like to move with the students to the High School program, or if they would like to take time off. This provides the volunteer with a clear understanding of what to expect and eliminates the feeling of being trapped forever.

Offer job rotation opportunities for variety or advancement. Consider opportunities to allow the volunteers to rotate responsibilities within their team or even rotating onto other teams. A volunteer that might be getting burned out with one role might discover they have a passion for another role they hadn't even considered.

Questions to Consider

- How can we be flexible if a volunteer cannot make a commitment on short notice?
- How can we provide a "leave of absence" if someone needs an extended period off from the commitment?
- How can we provide volunteers the ability to quit/leave/stop volunteering without feeling guilty?
- How can we rotate volunteer roles?
- How can you, as the leader, recognize if someone is feeling burn out?

Being Humble

"Title means nothing. The one with a servant's heart is the leader"

- unknown

Leading from the Front

Never ask someone to do a job you wouldn't do yourself. Be prepared to demonstrate you are not above any task - sweep a floor, load a truck, plunge a toilet. Be willing to do whatever it takes.

A few years ago, I received a mayday call from the operations manager of our food rescue non-profit. The driver scheduled to pick up several pallets of food from a large membership warehouse that day had called in sick. She called all of the backup volunteers and didn't have a driver. She knew three pantries were counting on the food involved, and she was desperate to find a solution. I told her to give me ten minutes, and I would call her back. I scurried down to my boss's office and requested the rest of the day off, which she quickly obliged. I headed for the parking garage and a 45-mile drive to pick up our refrigerated truck. When I called the operations manager to relay the plan, she was stunned. I had no other solutions, and time was of the essence. To me, that is leadership - the willingness to step into the gap whenever and wherever and say "Here I am. I can do it".

Habitat for Humanity demonstrates this every weekend during their builds. Their volunteers paint walls, hang sheetrock, and do a lot of things that they have never done before walking onto the job site. And the volunteer leaders never ask a volunteer to do anything that they themselves won't do. Often, they work right alongside the volunteers getting just as sweaty and worn out as the volunteers. I've watched them at lunch breaks stop eating midway through a sandwich, set their plate down, jump up and tie up a bag of garbage, put a new bag in the garbage can, haul off the bag of garbage, wash up, and then return to their lunch. The volunteers working with you will notice those same kinds of things. You might think they are trivial, but seeing a volunteer leader who is willing to do any task sets a good example and makes an indelible impression about your dedication.

Volunteers will follow you through a burning fire (both literally and figuratively), but only if they trust you. They will trust you when they see you genuinely have their best interest in mind, and they will do anything that you asked them to do. You need to be transparent and genuine. Admit your fears and shortcomings and be real with them.

In his inspiring book, The Catalyst Leader, Brad Lomenick says it simply, "Our organization doesn't need a leader with cool hair and skinny jeans. They need someone they can trust and follow. This can only happen if I embrace who I am rather than try to be someone else." (Lomevick, 2013)

"It is not fair to ask of others what you are not willing to do yourself."

- Eleanor Roosevelt

A Dash of Humility (Dan King)

With the success of quiz shows like "Are You Smarter Than a Fifth-Grader", it's evident that the idea of being "smarter than ___" is becoming increasingly important in our society.

These prime-time game shows are continually blasting us with the idea that success is somehow tied to how smart you are. "Who Wants to be a Millionaire" teaches us that knowing stuff can make you rich, while "The Weakest Link" further emphasizes the fact that being not as smart as the next guy is a problem.

I believe that *this mindset* is a problem, and as we continue through the Proverbs, I'd like to take this opportunity to discuss why I feel this way.

Solomon teaches us to, *"Trust in the Lord with all your heart, and do not lean on your own understanding"* (Proverbs 3:5).

There are two things that I feel like this passage teaches us. First, we need to trust the authority over us. Then second, we should not rely on our own knowledge and understanding.

What You Know

Solomon instructs us to, "not lean on our own understanding". There are a couple of things involved with this concept. First of all, relying on your own understanding or knowledge would require that you actually knew everything that you need to know. Rarely have I ever met anyone that actually knows everything that they need to know. (besides myself... okay, just kidding)

If this is the way that you're operating, then you're fooling yourself. Odds are that you actually don't know *EVERYTHING* you need to know. And if you think you do, then you probably could use a slice of humble pieto get over yourself.

Besides, even if you do know everything, then you may be denying the people around you from sharing something and feeling like they're a valuable member of "the community".

Building Community

Furthermore, relying on your own thoughts works against the idea of community that you should be building in your workplace (or volunteer organization). As a leader, you have a responsibility to build community with the people in your organization. Without this community effect, you will never get people to reach their full potential.

Therefore, if you're running around like Mr. Know-It-All, then you're likely snuffing out opportunities for others to get involved. Even if they share an idea that you already had, then at least you're allowing them the opportunity to feel like a valuable member of the community.

Relying on Our Authority

Then working backwards into this passage, we're also told to trust the Lord, who is our ultimate authority. In a business environment, I believe that this principle also requires us to trust those in authority over us.

However, when paired with the idea of not relying on your own understanding, then I think there's a respect principle that's being taught here that we shouldn't forget.

We should constantly be seeking the wisdom of our superiors and take what they share with us very seriously. This doesn't mean that you can't go to them with new and different ideas, because if they are also following this principle, then they wouldn't act as if they knew it all either.

What this means is that we need to engage in conversations with our superiors (who are more responsible for the vision of the organization more than we are), and respect what they have to offer us.

Questions to Consider

- How are you engaging those above you in conversations about how you can best affect the organization?

- Are you ready to hear anything they may have to say to you?

- What do you need to do to position yourself best for this conversation and respect their authority?

- What conversations are you having with the people below you?

- Are you acting like a know-it-all, or are you really open to hearing what they have to say?

- Try taking one of their ideas right now and implementing it, even if you "know" that it is going to fail. Seriously, what do you have to lose?

- By allowing that type of growth opportunity, what could you gain?

I believe that the smartest guy on the block is not the one who knows the most stuff, but is the one who knows how to use the resources around him/her in order to achieve the greatest level of success.

Addressing Volunteers as Investors Not Employees

"Volunteers are not servants. Volunteers are partners working together for improving America's future."

- Richard j. Daley, former mayor of Chicago

If you work for or operate a non-profit or even a church, consider something for a moment before addressing the volunteers. These aren't your paid employees. These aren't your personal servants. Chances are, these are people who regularly make financial contributions to the organization. And if so, these people are providing the money that goes into your paycheck. Some of the volunteers could even be members of the board of directors. Even if they are none of these, these volunteers are investing their time into your organization. They have taken a day out of their hectic lives to invest in the organization. How would you address a group of people who were investors in your company if you were a CEO of a large corporation? The Mr. and Mrs. titles would start getting used. Instead of barking orders, you would be asking, "Would you?" "Please" and "Thank You" would start being said more often. You should address your volunteers the same way.

I'm going to step on some toes here, so prepare yourself. Volunteers should be treated like investors. Volunteers should receive the better parking places. Volunteers should go through the lunch line first. If you want them coming back week after week and recruiting their friends as volunteers, you need to treat them as investors not as employees. We all tolerate a certain amount of bossiness from managers at our day jobs. We all tolerate their bad moods and gruff comments at least for a while, because we need the job to pay our bills. Volunteers are different. They don't need the role you are asking them to fill. They have no obligation to return next week. Bite their heads off or address them out of a position of superiority, and you will quickly be ready to change the name of your organization to JustUs.org. If you want them to give up a Saturday with their family after a long week at work, recognize their investment and address them with gratitude.

"Volunteers don't get paid, not because they're worthless, but because they're priceless.'

- Sherry Anderson

Listening

Ask Rather Than Tell

Give volunteers a real voice within the organization. The people in the trenches doing the work of the organization are the most familiar with what is going on in the day-to-day operations. They are our best source of information and feedback. If we don't provide them a voice, we are doing ourselves and our organization a disservice. We can make monumentally bad decisions based on our assumptions without the input of the volunteers. The people out in the parking lot quickly figure out what is wrong with the traffic flow or the method being used to park cars, because they are out there doing it day-in and day-out. We cannot make a good decision on how to direct traffic by assumptions or snap judgments. The ushers quickly understand how people respond to walking in the door of an auditorium and not finding an available seat and the impact it makes if we decide to eliminate two rows of chairs so it seems fuller. Before we decide to implement our next great idea, why don't we seek their input?

In The Catalyst Leader, Brad Lomenick writes, *"Be interested over interesting. Be more concerned with listening instead of talking. Focus on others, not yourself."* (Lomevick, 2013)

I will warn you though, if you are going to give them a voice, you better be prepared to accept when they tell you it is a bad idea or that you are wrong. Put the ego aside and do what is best for the organization and listen. You do not have to accept all their advice, but we owe it to them to at least listen to their input and consider it before making a final decision.

Joel Manby gives us this wisdom in his book Love Works, *"Leadership is a lonely business. When we rely on our own perspective, we miss our blind spots. We do the best we can, but if we have nobody telling us the truth, we will not improve over time."* (Manby, 2012)

If you remember nothing else from this chapter, I hope you will remember the Iceberg of Ignorance. In 1989, Sidney Yoshida published the results of an internationally acclaimed study conducted on mid-sized companies. Yoshida concluded: "Only 4% of an organization's front line problems are known by top management, 9% are known by middle management, 74% by supervisors and 100% by employees..."

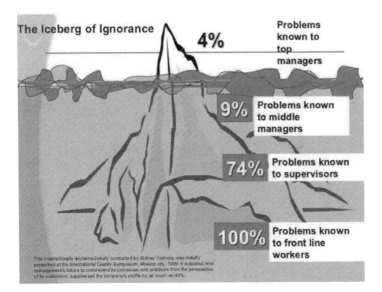

While there have been debates for and against the study's conclusions, it clearly demonstrates the need for us to openly discuss changes we are contemplating with the volunteers that the changes will affect.

Real, earnest listening makes the volunteer feel valued. As Max DePree notes, *"Dishonest or careless communication tells us as much about the people involved as it does about anything else. Communication is an ethical question. Good communication means a respect for individuals."* (DePree, 1987)

Have you ever had someone ask you for your input, and it quickly became obvious to you that they weren't listening? Or maybe they nod their head and act like they are listening, but really they are waiting to make their next point? Or maybe they are so distracted that they only hear every third or fourth word you speak, so when you are done talking, they cannot repeat what you just told them? How frustrating is that? I can't think of anything more frustrating than someone asking my advice on something I have experience in, and then they ignore the advice and make a costly mistake. It is so frustrating because we feel like they are discounting our worth and not valuing our input. And we feel like we have wasted our time trying to help by providing our personal insight and experience. As DePree points out, good listening communicates respect.

By listening to our volunteers, we can gain insight and wisdom, and possibly save ourselves and our team from a world of grief. I would rather learn from someone else's mistakes than have to suffer the scrapes and bruises of making all of the mistakes firsthand.

Greenleaf points out that listening provides wisdom: *"Listening is an attitude, an attitude toward other people and what they are trying to express. It begins with a genuine interest that is manifest in close attention, and it goes on to understanding in depth - whence cometh wisdom.* " (Greenleaf, 1977)

Listening Is Highly Underrated (Dan King)

After developing training for (and training) Customer Service Reps, I'm convinced that listening is a skill that does not get enough attention these days. There is nothing that says "you are important" more than truly listening to people. Listening says that you care about what someone has to say. You are putting their needs before your own.

Learn the art of asking questions and control yourself when people respond. Show them that you're listening by practicing active listening skills. I could write a whole series on the importance of listening, but for now just practice shutting your own mouth for a while and listening. If nothing else, you'll learn a lot and may be amazed at how much people will then want to hear what you think.

Questions to Consider

- How can you practice active listening in other conversations that you are having?

- Do you accept input from your volunteers without taking personal offense?

- What was the last suggestion a volunteer gave to you? Did you implement their idea?

- Do you carefully consider suggestions and find something useful in all of them?

- How can you make better decisions with input from the volunteers?

Demonstrating Appreciation

"Every single person you meet has a sign around his or her neck that says, 'make me feel important'. If you can do that, you'll be a success not only in business but in life as well"

– Mary Kay Ash

Give Credit Where Credit Is Due (Dan King)

Few things can crush a spirit more than the issue I'm about to discuss here.

Imagine getting assigned to a project that you've been dreaming about getting, and you pour your heart and soul into it. When it's complete, you step back and look at what you've done with a great sense of pride and accomplishment. You're proud of what you were able to do., and rightly so.

The big-wigs hear about this cool new thing going on and inquire about it. You can sense their pleasure with your new masterpiece!

Then it happens...

While standing at your desk with the executives gushing over your work, your boss speaks up and takes every bit of credit for the work that you've done. To add insult to injury, the executives congratulate your boss on a job well done, and never even glance in your direction again.

This actually happened to me twice.

Both times I felt absolutely miserable. I don't think I can recall any time in my professional life that I've felt so small and unappreciated. Most of us have probably been in this boat at one time or another in our lives.

Why is this so common? Because, generally speaking, people are selfish. We can probably wrap up this post by saying, "don't be selfish" and call it a day.

However, as I continue to look at Deborah in the Book of Judges (chapters 4 and 5), the next thing that I notice is that Deborah gave credit where credit was due.

In Judges 4:15, we first notice that the text is very clear about how the battle was won. Barak went out with 10,000 men following him into a battle that he was largely outmatched for, and the text states that, "the Lord routed Sisera and all his chariots and all his army."

Granted, I recognize that Barak was there, but it's important to notice that it must have been obvious that it was the Lord that caused them to succeed.

It's what happens after the battle was won that I find most interesting.

Deborah and Barak gave thanks and praise to the Lord for winning that battle. In other words, they gave credit where the credit was due.

You may also notice that Deborah even recognizes the efforts of the "commanders of Israel who offered themselves willingly". Basically, she gave credit up and down the chain of command. She gave credit everywhere it was due.

They could not have won that battle without either of those important elements, and Deborah recognized them both in her song and praises. But you'll also notice that Deborah never once took credit herself even though she had to lead them into battle.

A Sincere "Thank You" Goes a Long Way (Dan King)

I believe this is much more than simply expressing gratitude but is about helping others to feel important. People that earn respect not only know how to keep themselves down to earth, but also know how to lift others up.

Imagine this... you and your boss just got done working on a big project. When people start noticing it and complimenting it, how does it make you feel when your boss (who carried part of the load) responds to praises about the project with a, "thanks, but so-and-so (you) really carried this thing, and did a great job with it."? Especially if you're in earshot of that conversation, I'm sure it would raise your level of respect for your boss, simply because they made you feel valued.

Questions to Consider

- What victories are happening right now in your organization?

- How can you give credit *up* the chain of command?

- How do you think that attitude will affect other people in the organization? I'd bet that it would help to create an atmosphere of respect for superiors.

- Considering those same successes, how can you give credit *down* the chain of command?

- How do you think this will affect the attitude of the people you work with?

- If you do this, does it help or hurt your image as a leader in your organization?

Case Studies

Doing it Wrong

Case Study Number 1: The Seven Biggest Mistakes of A Self-Centered Leader (Dan King)

Succeeding in the workplace usually takes a great deal of talent. However, you can excel in all of the technical areas of your job but never see the advancement and growth within your organization if you don't have certain leadership qualities.

This is the case with Abimelech.

Abimelech was the son of Gideon (a.k.a. *Jerubbaal* which means "contender with Baal"), and his successor as Judge. Gideon was a great leader and had done a lot of good for Israel during his time.

Abimelech had a short reign as a judge, mostly because of his self-centeredness. Let's take a look at the mistakes that he made as he worked his way into leadership...

1. He had an unhealthy fixation on position

During this time of Israel's history, judges ruled the land. But as Abimelech took his leadership role, he had himself installed as a "king". But worse than that, he had just assumed that one (or all) of Gideon's sons would be Israel's next leader. To the best of my knowledge, the judges were not put in place by bloodline, but by God's appointment. So Abimelech had his sights set on a position that technically wasn't his, and even elevated it to a higher status than what it really was.

2. He thought more of himself than he ought (a.k.a. *arrogance*)

Of course he had all the skills that he needed. In fact, he was a great communicator As evidenced by his speech that he convinced people to move him into this role. But, if you have to convince people that you should be their leader, then you're not their leader. He was the son of the great Gideon, but so what? A dash of humility goes a long way!

3. He tuned out God (a.k.a. *disobedience*)

I know that for a non-religious reader, this one might not make much sense, but hear me out...

This may have been one of his biggest mistakes. God was the one that was in control of who gets leadership positions in ancient Israel. But Abimelech didn't bother to seek out God's direction or approval of this. Whether it's God in the religious sense, or the senior leadership of an organization, it's important to seek the counsel and approval of higher management and listen to what their will is. They're there for a reason.

4. He manipulated the system

I would never have my mom go into a job interview for me! But that's what Abimelech did! He convinced key members of his family to go for this crazy idea of his, and then sent his mom in to make the speech to the rest of the decision makers. I can just imagine this dude kicking back while he manipulates other people into getting him the job that he wanted. Actually, I've seen it happen at work too.

5. He failed to surround himself with the right people

The text indicates that he surrounded himself with "worthless and reckless men." If Abimelech wanted to grow into a great leader, then he needed to surround himself with other great people. We all know that we are (and become) like the people with whom we hang out with. Abimelech inevitably brought himself down by surrounding himself with the wrong people. Some people hang out with "lesser" people in order to help themselves feel elevated above others. I sense a little insecurity…

6. He forced his way into securing his leadership

This is probably one of the most repulsive things that Abimelech did. After stepping into his new job, he eliminated the competition. Literally, he killed all of his 70 brothers (one did get away) in order to get rid of any other claim to *his* throne. If you feel that threatened by other people, especially those closest to you, then you're probably not the right guy for the role. Again, doesn't this smell like insecurity?

7. He failed to think of long-term consequences

Abimelech's reign only lasted for three years, and God eventually had His say in the matter. The biggest problem with self-centeredness is that it's short-sighted. Abimelech's fight to get into the position caused him to only think about what it took to get there, and not the longer-term effects of his actions.

Pushing to get yourself into a position that you think you deserve may work for the short-term, but eventually people will catch on. Achieving solid, long-term success requires a selfless perspective and the heart of someone who simply wants what's best for the organization. If you approach it right, you may find yourself in a leadership role whether the title's there or not. *These* are the true leaders that make everything tick.

Case Study Number 2: Three Guaranteed Ways to Sabotage Your Influence (Dan King)

We all want our lives to have some sort of impact. If it's not in the workplace, then it may be at home with our kids, in the community, or in a variety of other places.

Wherever it is, the human condition causes us to have this deeply rooted need for our lives to actually mean something... to leave a legacy.

As Stephen Covey points out :

"There are certain things that are fundamental to human fulfillment. The essence of these needs is captured in the phrase 'to live, to love, to learn, to leave a legacy'... the need to leave a legacy is our spiritual need to have a sense of meaning, purpose, personal congruence, and contribution."

None of us wants to leave this world thinking that our lives meant nothing. So we strive to develop our legacy, and that happens through how well we influence others here and now.

The test of how well we do in this aspect of our lives happens well after we're gone. As we continue with studying lessons from leaders, we come to the account of Tola and Jair as recorded in Judges 10:1-6.

Here we have two leaders of Israel who had virtually nothing recorded about their reigns. Each had ruled for over 20 years, but neither left a worthwhile legacy for the nation of Israel to pass down as the other Judges did. Let's take a look at three ways that we can identify from the text that they sabotaged their own influence and legacy...

1. Failure to Develop Others

One of the things that's apparent from the text is that there's no mention of other people that they helped to develop into future leaders. If we truly want to have an influence on others, then we must take the time to teach them and develop them to pick up wherever we leave off. When I think about this principle, I most easily see it illustrated in the life of my son. When I take the time to teach him important life skills, a piece of me ends up living on through him. Failing to take the time to develop other people will guarantee that you have no impact through them.

2. Have a Short-Sighted Vision

While both of these men had very successful and long reigns, neither of them thought about the future after they were gone. The text continues after Jair's death with the statement that, "then the children of Israel again did evil in the sight of the Lord" (v.6). It's apparent that they worked to keep things running smoothly while they were there but did not work to ensure that the people would continue to do good after they were gone. A great leader will think longer-term than what the immediate situation calls for.

3. Focus Only on Reputation

The fact that nothing negative was recorded about these men leads me to believe that they actually had a good reputation. There wasn't anything bad to say about them. But is this enough? Isn't that really settling for mediocrity? When the history of your life, job, family, etc. is written, would you want it to appear like the records of Tola and Jair? You may never give anyone a reason to say anything bad about you now, but are you giving them reason enough to say something about who you were and what you stood for once you're gone?

For my final thought on this topic, I leave you with another quote. Legendary evangelist Billy Graham said,

"Our days are numbered. One of the primary goals in our lives should be to prepare for our last day. The legacy we leave is not just in our possessions, but in the quality of our lives. What preparations should we be making now? The greatest waste in all of our earth, which cannot be recycled or reclaimed, is our waste of the time that God has given us each day."

Doing it Right

Case Study Number 3: Jesus - The Original Servant Leader

In this case study, we will not argue theology or the deity of Jesus. What we are focusing on is his modeling of servant leadership. If you don't believe in Jesus as the Savior, view this from the perspective of history and the lessons in leadership that we can gain from it.

From the start, Jesus made his humility in his role as a leader crystal clear. He put others first, choosing not to be served, but to serve. When two of the disciples began to quarrel about position and rank, Jesus reset their focus.

"You've observed how godless rulers throw their weight around," he said, *"and when people get a little power how quickly it goes to their heads. It's not going to be that way with you. Whoever wants to be great must become a servant. Whoever wants to be first among you must be your slave. That is what the Son of Man has done: He came to serve, not to be served—and then to give away his life in exchange for many who are held hostage."* (Mark 10:41-45, The Message)

He directly addressed humility.

"Do you want to stand out? Then step down. Be a servant. If you puff yourself up, you'll get the wind knocked out of you. But if you're content to simply be yourself, your life will count for plenty. (Matthew 23:11-12, The Message)

He clearly demonstrated his humility as a servant leader when he washed the disciples' feet.

So he got up from the supper table, set aside his robe, and put on an apron. Then he poured water into a basin and began to wash the feet of the disciples, drying them with his apron. (John 13:3-5, The Message)

As the leader of a group of volunteers, Jesus performed several notable leadership functions:

• **He communicated his vision**

Jesus was very clear time and time again that he came to draw people to God. The religious leaders of the time constantly complained about the company he kept.

Later when Jesus was eating supper at Matthew's house with his close followers, a lot of disreputable characters came and joined them. When the Pharisees saw him keeping this kind of company, they had a fit, and lit into Jesus' followers. "What kind of example is this from your Teacher, acting cozy with crooks and riffraff?"

Jesus, overhearing, shot back, "Who needs a doctor: the healthy or the sick? Go figure out what this Scripture means: 'I'm after mercy, not religion.' I'm here to invite outsiders, not coddle insiders." (Matthew 9:10-13, The Message)

- He focused on the mission

We see very clearly how laser focused Jesus was on his mission when the devil tempted him for 40 days and nights. He was tempted to turn a stone into bread when he was hungry, but responded by referencing scripture in Deuteronomy , *"It takes more than bread to really live."* (Luke 4:4). When he was tempted to worship the devil, he responded *"Worship the Lord your God and only the Lord your God. Serve him with absolute single-heartedness."* (Luke 4:8). When tempted to leap from the top of the temple, he refused saying *" it's also written, 'Don't you dare tempt the Lord your God.'"* (Luke 4:12, The Message)

- He valued people

Jesus outlined how his volunteers should posture themselves when he said, *"Love the Lord your God with all your passion and prayer and intelligence.' This is the most important, the first on any list. But there is a second to set alongside it:*

'Love others as well as you love yourself.' These two commands are pegs; everything in God's Law and the Prophets hangs from them.' (Matthew 22:39-40, The Message)

And he walked the talk. He ate with sinners. He hung out with the marginalized. He stood up for the accused. Remember Zacchaeus, the short despised tax collector? Jesus sought him out and exalted him among his enemies. *Then Jesus entered and walked through Jericho. There was a man there, his name Zacchaeus, the head tax man and quite rich. He wanted desperately to see Jesus, but the crowd was in his way—he was a short man and couldn't see over the crowd. So he ran on ahead and climbed up in a sycamore tree so he could see Jesus when he came by.*

When Jesus got to the tree, he looked up and said, "Zacchaeus, hurry down. Today is my day to be a guest in your home." Zacchaeus scrambled out of the tree, hardly believing his good luck, delighted to take Jesus home with him. Everyone who saw the incident was indignant and grumped, "What business does he have getting cozy with this crook?"

Zacchaeus just stood there, a little stunned. He stammered apologetically, "Master, I give away half my income to the poor—and if I'm caught cheating, I pay four times the damages."

Jesus said, "Today is salvation day in this home! Here he is: Zacchaeus, son of Abraham! For the Son of Man came to find and restore the lost." (Luke 19:1-10, the Message)

• He trained and empowered

He taught and trained non-stop.

When the Sabbath arrived, Jesus lost no time in getting to the meeting place. He spent the day there teaching. They were surprised at his teaching—so forthright, so confident—not quibbling and quoting like the religious scholar. (Mark 1:21-22, The Message)

When Jesus arrived, he saw this huge crowd. At the sight of them, his heart broke—like sheep with no shepherd they were. He went right to work teaching them. (Mark 6:34, The Message)

He gathered his team together, empowered them with his authority, and sent them on their mission.

Jesus called his twelve disciples to him and gave them authority to drive out impure spirits and to heal every disease and sickness. (Matthew 10:1, The Message)

- He supported his team

After giving them their marching orders, Jesus told him he would be with them. He had their backs, now and going forward.

Jesus, undeterred, went right ahead and gave his charge: "God authorized and commanded me to commission you: Go out and train everyone you meet, far and near, in this way of life, marking them by baptism in the threefold name: Father, Son, and Holy Spirit. Then instruct them in the practice of all I have commanded you. I'll be with you as you do this, day after day after day, right up to the end of the age." (Matthew 28:20, The Message)

- He spoke into the chaos around him

He didn't get caught up in the storms of life and let them distract him from his mission. Instead he spoke into the chaos and told it to shut up.

One day he and his disciples got in a boat. "Let's cross the lake," he said. And off they went. It was smooth sailing, and he fell asleep. A terrific storm came up suddenly on the lake. Water poured in, and they were about to capsize. They woke Jesus: "Master, Master, we're going to drown!"

Getting to his feet, he told the wind, "Silence!" and the waves, "Quiet down!" They did it. The lake became smooth as glass. (Luke 8:22-24, the Message)

- He attended to immediate needs

When a leaper approached Jesus and asked for healing, he healed him immediately. He didn't say, "Now is not a good time" or "Can you come back during office hours".

Jesus came down the mountain with the cheers of the crowd still ringing in his ears. Then a leper appeared and went to his knees before Jesus, praying, "Master, if you want to, you can heal my body."

Jesus reached out and touched him, saying, "I want to. Be clean." Then and there, all signs of the leprosy were gone. Jesus said, "Don't talk about this all over town. Just quietly present your healed body to the priest, along with the appropriate expressions of thanks to God. Your cleansed and grateful life, not your words, will bear witness to what I have done." (Matthew 8:1-4, The Message)

When the crowds approached, he immediately healed the sick and when they became hungry, he fed them.

Soon a lot of people from the nearby villages walked around the lake to where he was. When he saw them coming, he was overcome with pity and healed their sick.

Toward evening the disciples approached him. "We're out in the country and it's getting late. Dismiss the people so they can go to the villages and get some supper."

But Jesus said, "There is no need to dismiss them. You give them supper."

"All we have are five loaves of bread and two fish," they said.

Jesus said, "Bring them here." Then he had the people sit on the grass. He took the five loaves and two fish, lifted his face to heaven in prayer, blessed, broke, and gave the bread to the disciples. The disciples then gave the food to the congregation. They all ate their fill. They gathered twelve baskets of leftovers. About five thousand were fed. (Matthew 14:14-21, The Message)

- He worked to bring about change

He went toe to toe with the religious leaders of the day and addressed their piety.

"You're hopeless, you religion scholars and Pharisees! Frauds! You keep meticulous account books, tithing on every nickel and dime you get, but on the meat of God's Law, things like fairness and compassion and commitment—the absolute

basics—you carelessly take it or leave it. Careful bookkeeping is commendable, but the basics are required. Do you have any idea how silly you look, writing a life story that's wrong from start to finish, nitpicking over commas and semicolons?" (Matthew 23:23-24, The Message)

When the Pharisees, a money-obsessed bunch, heard him say these things, they rolled their eyes, dismissing him as hopelessly out of touch. So Jesus spoke to them: "You are masters at making yourselves look good in front of others, but God knows what's behind the appearance. What society sees and calls monumental, God sees through and calls monstrous. God's Law and the Prophets climaxed in John; Now it's all kingdom of God— the glad news and compelling invitation to every man and woman. The sky will disintegrate and the earth dissolve before a single letter of God's Law wears out. Using the legalities of divorce as a cover for lust is adultery; Using the legalities of marriage as a cover for lust is adultery." (Luke 16:14-18, The Message)

- He endured betrayal, hatred, and the harsh scrutiny of the old guard

"If you find the godless world is hating you, remember it got its start hating me. If you lived on the world's terms, the world would love you as one of its own. But since I picked you to live on God's

terms and no longer on the world's terms, the world is going to hate you." (John 15:18-19, The Message)

After raising Lazarus from the dead, the religious leaders of the day were livid.

That was a turnaround for many of the Jews who were with Mary. They saw what Jesus did, and believed in him. But some went back to the Pharisees and told on Jesus. The high priests and Pharisees called a meeting of the Jewish ruling body. "What do we do now?" they asked. "This man keeps on doing things, creating God-signs. If we let him go on, pretty soon everyone will be believing in him and the Romans will come and remove what little power and privilege we still have."

Then one of them—it was Caiaphas, the designated Chief Priest that year—spoke up, "Don't you know anything? Can't you see that it's to our advantage that one man dies for the people rather than the whole nation be destroyed?" He didn't say this of his own accord, but as Chief Priest that year he unwittingly prophesied that Jesus was about to die sacrificially for the nation, and not only for the nation but so that all God's exile-scattered children might be gathered together into one people.

From that day on, they plotted to kill him. (John 11:45-54, The Message)

And one of his closest team members betrayed him.

So Judas led the way to the garden, and the Roman soldiers and police sent by the high priests and Pharisees followed. They arrived there with lanterns and torches and swords. Jesus, knowing by now everything that was coming down on him, went out and met them. (John 18:2-4, The Message)

- He forgave

Even as he was being crucified, Jesus forgave a criminal hanging on a cross just off to one side.

One of the criminals hanging alongside cursed him: "Some Messiah you are! Save yourself! Save us!"

But the other one made him shut up: "Have you no fear of God? You're getting the same as him. We deserve this, but not him—he did nothing to deserve this."

Then he said, "Jesus, remember me when you enter your kingdom."

He said, "Don't worry, I will. Today you will join me in paradise." (Luke 23:39-43, The Message)

And while the soldiers who hung him on the cross stood and mocked him and gambled to divide up his clothing, he prayed for them, *"Father,*

forgive them. They don't know what they're doing."
(Luke 23:34, The Message)

Case Study Number 4: Truett Cathy - A Servant Leader in the Business World

Truett Cathy was born into poverty in Atlanta in 1921. His father had suffered financial loss during the Great Depression that deeply affected him emotionally. Truett's mother took in boarders to make ends meet and as a child, Truett worked to bring extra income into the household selling Coca-Cola, newspapers, and any odd job he could find. After serving in the Army, Truett returned to Atlanta and opened the Dwarf House Grill - a tiny restaurant with only four booths and 10 stools at the counter.

In 1961, Truett created a pressure-cooked chicken filet sandwich which soon became his trademark. In 1967, he launched his first Chick-fil-A restaurant, in the Greenbriar Mall in Atlanta - the first major shopping mall on the south side of Atlanta and the second enclosed mall in the state. Over the next 20 years the business would develop into a major food chain. Truett held to his early principles valuing people over profits and continued his tradition of closing his business on Sundays. He developed programs to train staff for management positions and provided opportunities for them to become franchise owners.

For decades, Truett led a Sunday School class for 13 year old boys and he and his wife took in more than 150 foster children. (Dobbs)

By 1984, he launched the WinShape Center Foundation to shape winners of young people by helping them succeed in life through scholarships and support programs. WinShape Center Foundation now awards more than 20 scholarships worth up to $32,000. He also established WinShape Homes, 14 foster homes (nine in Georgia, three in Tennessee, one in Alabama, and one in Brazil), to provide a safe, caring and stable home environment for children. (About Winshape)

Truett Cathy died on September 8, 2014 at the age of 93. At the time of his death, Chi-fil-A was the number one chicken chain in the United States with 1,800 locations and sales exceeding $5 billion. His net worth at the time of his death was $6.2 billion according to Forbes magazine who listed him as number 68 on the Forbes 400 list in 2013. (Profile - S. Truett Cathy)

Dave Ramsey summed up seven lessons we can learn from Truett Cathy's life and servant leadership style:

1. Define your values and stick to them
2. A little customer service goes a long way
3. Make family a priority
4. Know why you exist

5. Plan ahead
6. Invest in others
7. Don't be afraid to start small

(Ramsey)

Why Volunteers Quit

A recent article in The Journal of Volunteer Administration indicates that one of the principal reasons people leave their volunteer positions is that they feel unappreciated and unrecognized. This seems like a relatively easy thing to resolve. This is the key to retaining volunteers we have worked so hard to recruit and train - ensure they feel appreciated and that their commitment and service is recognized.

The Top Ten Reasons Why Volunteers Leave Unexpectedly

Reason no. 10

The reality of their experience was not what they expected when they signed on.

Reason no. 9

Employees treated them as an interruption, not as welcome help.

Reason no. 8

Veteran long-term volunteers wouldn't let them into their "insider" group.

Reason no. 7

They did not see the connection between one day's work and another.

Reason no. 6

They did not know how to tell you they wanted to leave.

Reason no. 5

They made a suggestion that was not acted on or responded to.

Reason no. 4

The atmosphere was impersonal, tense or cold.

Reason no. 3

The physical environment did not support their efforts.

Reason no. 2

No one smiled at them.

Reason no. 1

They were underutilized.

Questions to Consider

- How can you develop others?
- How can you ensure you are not operating with a short-sighted vision?
- How can you stay focused on the vision and mission and not worry about your reputation?
- How can you ensure your volunteers feel appreciated?
- How can you ensure that new volunteers are included and not made to feel like an outsider?
- Are you being transparent with new recruits regarding the tasks you are asking them to undertake?

Bibliography

About Winshape. (n.d.). Retrieved from Winshape.org: https://winshape.org/about/

DePree, M. (1987). *Leadership is an Art.* East Lansing, Michigan: Michigan State University Press.

Dobbs, C. (n.d.). *Truett Cathy (1921-2014).* Retrieved from New Georgia Encyclopedia: https://www.georgiaencyclopedia.org/articles/business-economy/truett-cathy-1921-2014

Greenleaf, R. K. (1977). *Servant Leadership.* Mahwah: Paulist Press.

Lomevick, B. (2013). *The Catalyst Leader.* Nashville: Thomas Nelson, Inc.

Manby, J. (2012). *Love Works.* Grand Rapids: Zondervan.

Profile - S. Truett Cathy. (n.d.). Retrieved from Forbes.com: https://www.forbes.com/profile/s-truett-cathy/

Ramsey, D. (n.d.). *7 Life Lessons from Truett Cathy.* Retrieved from daveramsey.com:

https://www.daveramsey.com/blog/7-life-lessons-from-truett-cathy

Additional Resources and Recommended Reading

Visit allenmadding.com/p/volunteer-management-resources.html for additional resources and a list of recommended reading on the subject of Volunteer Management.

Other Books By Allen Madding

Shaken Awake

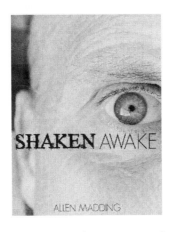

"Shaken Awake!" is the story of a church in downtown Atlanta, Georgia faced with a dwindling and aging congregation that has been forced to shut down the majority of their building and dismissed much of its staff. With limited funds, they shutter all of their ministries and programs leaving only a couple adult Sunday School classes and a Sunday morning worship service. When a homeless man freezes to death on the steps of their sanctuary, the church begins to re-examine their mission and priorities.

Awakened

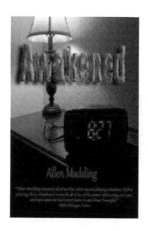

The sequel to "Shaken Awake!", "Awakened" picks up where the story leaves off. Peachtree Street Church has slowly been dwindling away as it members have died. In the face of a winter storm, the pastor and a small group of people open the doors of their fellowship hall and education wing to the homeless and those stranded and seeking shelter from the cold. The experience opens their eyes to the plight of the homeless living just outside the doors of their church. They begin to search for meaningful ways to effectively make a difference in the lives of their community one person at a time. The journey takes them farther than they ever imagined and completely changes the trajectory of their lives in the process.

Other Books by Dan King

The Unlikely Missionary: From Pew-Warmer to Poverty-Fighter

At some point in their life, most Christians have walked through the doors of their church on Sunday morning and wondered what it really means to live a Christian life. Unfortunately, few ever do more than warm a pew on Sunday and try to be a *"good person"* throughout the week. But the reality is Jesus called us to change the world starting with 'the least of these.'

Activist Faith: From Him and For Him
by Dillon Burroughs, Dan King, Daniel Darling

Join the cofounders of the dynamic Activist Faith movement (ActivistFaith.org) as they shine the light on Christians who are moving beyond politics and opinion to actively engage 12 divisive social issues. Activist Faith shares biblical contexts, personal stories, and practical guidance for a new generation of Christian activists.

Made in the USA
Columbia, SC
09 January 2019